Mythical Creatures

MERMAIDS

by Theresa Jarosz Alberti

FOCUS READERS

FOCUS READERS

www.focusreaders.com

Focus Readers is distributed by North Star Editions:
sales@northstareditions.com | 888-417-0195

Produced for Focus Readers by Red Line Editorial.

Photographs ©: Toporkova/Shutterstock Images, cover, 1; Yuri_Arcurs/iStockphoto, 4–5; duncan1890/iStockphoto, 7; Yodchai Prominn/Shutterstock Images, 8–9; Glevalex/Shutterstock Images, 11; volkova natalia/Shutterstock Images, 13; Andrea Izzotti/Shutterstock Images, 14–15, 22–23, 29; Chris Cornish/Shutterstock Images, 17; Kent Weakley/Shutterstock Images, 19; Zhu huanan/Imaginechina/AP Images, 20–21; ZU_09/iStockphoto, 25; rudall30/iStockphoto, 26

ISBN
978-1-63517-902-6 (hardcover)
978-1-64185-004-9 (paperback)
978-1-64185-206-7 (ebook pdf)
978-1-64185-105-3 (hosted ebook)

Library of Congress Control Number: 2018931680

Printed in the United States of America
Mankato, MN
April, 2019

About the Author

Theresa Jarosz Alberti called herself a writer when she was 10 years old. She wrote many stories and poems. Now she enjoys writing for both kids and adults. She lives in Minneapolis, Minnesota.

TABLE OF CONTENTS

CHAPTER 1

In the Deep Blue Sea 5

CHAPTER 2

Mermaids in History 9

CHAPTER 3

Maybe a Manatee 15

EXPLORING THE MYTH

Mermaids Today 20

CHAPTER 4

Under Waves or on Land 23

Focus on Mermaids • 28

Glossary • 30

To Learn More • 31

Index • 32

CHAPTER 1

IN THE DEEP BLUE SEA

When morning comes, the mermaid smiles. She plans her day. First, she will pick a bouquet of beautiful **sea anemones**. Then, she will play with the dolphins. The coral **reef** is also fun to visit.

Mermaids spend most of their time deep below the water's surface.

She loves to see the dazzling colors and shapes.

But first, the mermaid swims above the waves and looks around. She does this every morning. Today, she sees a big ship. Then she notices a boy in the water. He is sinking!

FUN FACT

In some stories, mermaids are immortal. This means they can live forever.

A mermaid saves a human boy in the sea.

Normally, the mermaid hides from humans. Yet she knows she must help. After saving the boy, she will disappear once again.

CHAPTER 2

MERMAIDS IN HISTORY

Oceans are huge and mysterious. Today, scientists have tools to explore the water. They use **scuba gear** and cameras. But in the past, humans did not have these tools.

Mermaid statues are popular around the world. This one is in Thailand.

They wondered what lived in the water. Many people believed in mermaids.

The word mermaid comes from two old words. *Mere* means "sea," and *maid* means "girl." Put together, *mermaid* means "girl of the sea." The words *mermen* and *merfolk* also describe the mythical creatures. *Mermen* describes males, and *merfolk* describes all genders.

In stories, Oannes was the first merman. This ancient god was half

Atargatis appears on this ancient coin from Greece.

man and half fish. The goddess Atargatis was half woman and half fish. She was the first mermaid.

Greek **myths** include many tales of merfolk. The god Triton was a merman. He used a **trident** to control the sea. Myths also told of sirens. A siren was half woman and half bird. In later stories, sirens looked like mermaids. They **inspired** many mermaid tales.

FUN FACT

The *Odyssey* is a long Greek poem from the 700s BCE. It was the first story to mention sirens.

This statue in Saint Petersburg, Russia, shows Triton battling a dragon.

In 1836, Hans Christian Andersen wrote *The Little Mermaid*. In this tale, a mermaid wants to become human. Many movies are based on this popular story.

CHAPTER 3

MAYBE A MANATEE

A mermaid is human from the waist up. From the waist down, she is a fish. She has a large, shiny tail covered in **scales**. These scales can be many colors.

In stories, mermaids live alongside other sea creatures.

Most mermaids are beautiful. They have long, flowing hair. Sometimes, they wear shells or coral. Mermaids collect these items as jewelry. In many stories, mermaids carry a mirror and comb. They are often vain. They like to look at their reflections. They also like to brush their hair.

FUN FACT

In some myths, mermaids have green, tangled hair. It is made of seaweed and kelp.

Some mermaids have brightly colored hair, skin, and eyes.

Mermen are similar to mermaids. They also have long hair. Some have beards, too. Most mermen are large and strong.

The appearance of mermaids depends on the story. In Irish myths, mermaids and mermen are called merrows. The female merrow has pale skin and dark eyes. The male merrow has green skin, hair, and teeth. He also has webbed fingers.

FUN FACT

Japanese folklore tells of mermaid-like creatures called kappa. The kappa is a water spirit. It has an ape-like face and a turtle-like shell.

Swimming manatees may look similar to mermaids.

Some sea creatures look a bit like mermaids from stories. The explorer Christopher Columbus thought he saw a mermaid. Experts think he saw a manatee or a dugong. These sea animals have large tails.

MERMAIDS TODAY

Some people like to dress up as mermaids. They buy tails made from fabric or **silicone**. The tails can weigh as much as 45 pounds (20 kg). The best tails are very expensive. They allow humans to swim like mermaids.

Hundreds of people in the United States work as mermaids. They perform shows in water. Professional mermaids must be able to swim well. They need to hold their breath for a long time. Some **aquariums** have mermaid shows. Mermaids and mermen dive for audiences. They may even swim with sea animals such as stingrays and sharks.

A professional mermaid performs in a show in China.

CHAPTER 4

UNDER WAVES OR ON LAND

Mermaids make their homes in the ocean. Some live alone in sea caves. Others live in underwater kingdoms. They belong to a community of merfolk.

A mermaid leaves her cave to explore the sea.

Mermaids are musical creatures. They love to sing. Some mermaids use their singing to trick humans. Sirens sing magical songs to attract sailors. The sailors follow the music. Then, the sirens **drown** them in the water.

FUN FACT

Mami Wata is a spirit in African myths. She often takes the form of a mermaid. She can bring both bad and good luck.

Sirens call out to a group of sailors.

Other mermaids are kind. They are interested in humans. Some help humans who are in danger.

Mermaids take breaks from swimming by sitting on rocks.

However, mermaids can also be shy. They often hide from humans.

In European folklore, selkies are similar to mermaids. In water, selkies appear as seals. But on land, they lose their seal skin. They become humans. They fall in love and have families. But soon, they miss the water. If a selkie's husband finds the seal skin, he hides it. Otherwise, the selkie will put it on. She will become a seal and return to the sea.

FUN FACT

In 2013, a TV channel made a fake news show about mermaids. Afterwards, many people were confused. They thought mermaids might be real.

FOCUS ON

MERMAIDS

Write your answers on a separate piece of paper.

1. Write a sentence describing one mermaid trait from Chapter 4.
2. Would you rather meet a mermaid, a selkie, or a siren? Why?
3. Which sea animal did Christopher Columbus possibly mistake for a mermaid?
   - A. a shark
   - B. a stingray
   - C. a dugong
4. Besides having a tail, how are mermaids similar to fish?
   - A. They have long hair.
   - B. They have two arms.
   - C. They have scales.

5. What does **vain** mean in this book?

*They are often **vain**. They like to look at their reflections. They also like to brush their hair.*

A. proud of the way one looks
B. afraid to look in a mirror
C. able to grow long hair

6. What does **attract** mean in this book?

*Sirens sing magical songs to **attract** sailors. The sailors follow the music.*

A. to bring in
B. to send away
C. to let go of

Answer key on page 32.

GLOSSARY

aquariums
Tanks of water that people keep animals in.

drown
To cause someone or something to die by holding it underwater.

inspired
Influenced or brought about.

myths
Well-known, fictional stories common to a group of people.

reef
A ridge of rock, coral, or sand just below the ocean surface.

scales
The thin, flat, overlapping pieces of hard skin that cover the bodies of fish and reptiles.

scuba gear
Tools that help people dive and breathe underwater.

sea anemones
Sea animals that look like flowers.

silicone
A tough, human-made substance.

trident
A spear with three points.

TO LEARN MORE

BOOKS

Goddu, Krystyna Poray. *Sea Monsters: From Kraken to Nessie*. Minneapolis: Lerner Publications, 2017.

Gregory, Josh. *Seals*. New York: Children's Press, 2015.

Sautter, A. J. *A Field Guide to Elves, Dwarves, and Other Magical Folk*. Mankato, MN: Capstone Press, 2015.

NOTE TO EDUCATORS

Visit **www.focusreaders.com** to find lesson plans, activities, links, and other resources related to this title.

INDEX

A

Andersen, Hans Christian, 13
Atargatis, 11

C

Columbus, Christopher, 19

D

dugong, 19

H

humans, 9, 13, 15, 20, 24–27

K

kappa, 18

L

Little Mermaid, 13

M

Mami Wata, 24
manatee, 19
merfolk, 10, 12, 23
mermen, 10, 17–18, 20
merrows, 18

O

Oannes, 10

S

selkies, 26–27
sirens, 12, 24

T

tails, 15, 19, 20
Triton, 12

Answer Key: 1. Answers will vary; **2.** Answers will vary; **3.** C; **4.** C; **5.** A; **6.** A